MOMXIETY

A TRUE STORY ABOUT THE MOTHER OF ALL
ANXIETIES.

JEN WESTBY

COPYRIGHT

DEDICATION

Dedication: To moms who worry and creatively imagine all, "what if" scenarios. You're definitely not alone.

CHAPTER ONE

GOODBYE FRIEND.

The sudden onset of symptoms led me to believe something was tragically wrong with me. It was almost like I went from feeling like me—normal mid twenty-year-old, who started dating this wonderful guy named Keith, going on trips, working full time, great life, you name it. To feeling like my life was limited down to minutes and seconds due to real, scary symptoms that magically appeared.

This literally happened overnight. There wasn't one thing I could think of that made all of this happen. I wasn't stressed out, nor having something negative affecting my life. In all honesty, my life was probably at its best. I wish there was one thing I could put my finger on to attach what was happening to me. It would have been much easier to think, "Oh, this is why I feel this way, because (Blank) happened. Nope, there was nothing. Just waves of emotions, mental symptoms, and body symptoms.

I felt like I was having heart attacks, and strokes, sometimes at the same time. I would get dizzy and feel light-headed—so naturally I thought I had a brain tumor. I also felt like I could pass out, all the time. I was literally scared out of my mind. My chest would get tight. I'd have a heaviness around my collarbones and felt like I had to take note of my breathing. I had vision issues, sometimes it would be too bright, or too dark. Then the tunnel vision would happen on occasion as these waves of symptoms would appear and send me down a negative road of fear and paralyze my functionality in its path.

This was only a drop in the bucket of what I was going through or about to go through, really.

Having nothing to tie to what was happening to me, brought on fears that there was a massive health issue going on and I needed help.

I began seeing my family doctor, who unfortunately wasn't much help at all. She seemed to discount my words and not take me seriously. Which pissed me off. Generally, before this health crisis, I was outgoing but shy, I was the apologizer and I certainly didn't have a backbone to stand up for myself like I should have. However, when you become scared and fearful, things change.

I went to so many doctor's appointments that I could hear the agony in the receptionist's voice when I said my name to schedule. I think I had a blue dot or something on my chart that alerted them of this crazy girl who keeps calling and thinking something is wrong. I'm sure the word "hypochondriac" was used in association with my name. But I couldn't give zero fucks about it. If they wanted to label me, fine, but if they could stand in my body for two hours, they would be eating crow.

The doctor humored me with a few blood tests, which was awesome when a nurse nicked my vein and immediately sent pins and needles down my arm. Now I had another worry to add to my growing list of symptoms, feelings, emotions, and fear.

As my life seemed to change drastically, I had just about every test done. From Echo Cardio Gram's, to MRI's, to more blood tests and even a trip to a neurologist, which I was *hoping* that would tell me that I'm losing it, just so I could have a diagnosis as to what the hell was going on with me.

Everything changed and came crashing down the day before Thanksgiving in 2003. I was headed into my work at a local Dodge,

Chrysler Jeep dealership in Renton, WA. I left my house with the heat on, but my window cracked for fresh air. For some reason, it just made sense at the time and made me feel like I could get air, that was the normal routine. Even on the cold, Fall mornings.

But I just felt off. I couldn't put my finger on it, just not the same old Jen I had grown to miss over the last few weeks. As I entered the freeway for the longer part of my commute, I was startled by the way my legs cramped and shook. I recall looking down at them as if they were someone else's legs and feet somehow attached to my body, and I didn't control their movements. I took the next exit I could and called Keith who was at home getting ready for work. He said to take some deep breaths and come back home. He would wait for me to get there and go in late to work.

By the time I was back onto the freeway in the opposite direction heading toward home, my legs were shaking so bad I couldn't keep a consistent speed, my heart was racing, I was beginning to feel light-headed and knew it was time to call 911. Interestingly enough, a police officer had someone pulled over on the side of the freeway. My initial thought was to pull over and have him help me, but my reaction kept me going. I didn't want to embarrass myself, and besides, he was busy. Never mind the thought process of me dying rolling through my head, "but he's busy, I don't want to bother him" was the thought that was louder. I'm sure the person who he pulled over would have rather had a distraction of me and my shaking legs than a speeding ticket. But it wasn't their lucky day.

By this time, the towel needed to be thrown in and I had called 911 for medical help. I exited off the freeway and pulled over to the side of the road next to a restaurant where an ambulance, fire truck and battalion chief met me with their flashing lights and vocal sirens. I'm sure the customers at the Shari's restaurant didn't expect free entertainment with their breakfast, but who am I to disappoint.

The battalion chief opened my passenger door and reached in to check the pulse on my right arm. "Are you okay? You look pale."

With a blank stare, I said, "I don't know what is wrong with me."

He helped me out of my car and escorted me to the ambulance where they plugged me into the heart monitor. Just about this time is when my cell phone rang, and it hit me I didn't call Keith back. I called him before 911 to say I was coming home and something was very wrong with me. However, the nice paramedic fielded that call and informed him I was being taken to the emergency room. Apparently, because of my symptoms, that were easing by now, I had to be seen. One of the fire fighters moved my Ford Expedition off the side of the road as I was being strapped in the first ride in an ambulance. Which by the way, isn't so much fun going down a steep hill feeling like you're going to tip over backwards. Plus, the damn bed kept clanging and banging from the bumps in the roads, which embarrassed me to no end. I couldn't understand why I felt like I was being too much trouble.

Once into the Emergency Room, I was given their oh-so-glamorous hospital jammies, which as we all know, leave a cool breeze on the back end. Then I was offered some juice, which I happily squirted down the front of me, leading me to believe I'm regressing to become a toddler, so yes, something is up with me and my out-of-reality body and mind symptoms.

After an EKG, a chat with the nurse and finally the Doctor, I was sent on my way with a prescription of Xanax, and really no answer to what happened to me, other than, "this will help your anxiety." What anxiety? You mean the leg shaking, tunnel vision, massive heart rate increase, fearing that I'm going to pass out and die, is anxiety? Nope. I wasn't buying it, and I didn't fill the prescription either. A medical issue was happening to me and they wanted to just slap a prescription in my hand and send me on my way. Fearing that this would happen to me again, since it was so out of the blue and sudden, my life came down to living in full fear. Fear of the unknown. Fear of, "oh no, this twinge in my body feels funny, is this what is wrong with me?" Or, "that head pain felt funny, am I having a stroke?" It's interesting how you can go from no fear of life, to instantly worrying about your life. It was like a switch was flipped and my new normal was anything but that.

After the episode of what they called, "Anxiety..." I found myself in a lifestyle that was new and full of health worries and fears. Gone were the days of waking up and being excited about an upcoming trip or weekend adventure, not to mention date night. Keith and I had a wonderful life of travel and fun experiences. It was something I've always wanted to do with someone, and I finally met him.

Now, I woke up fearing what symptoms I would have that day, and would I be able to make it through a day without having to go home, call the doctor or go to an emergency room. I remember going up to Monroe, WA to watch ATV flat track races, and sitting in the stands feeling like it was hard to breath. I checked my pulse and was very aware of my breaths. If it felt, "off" I started to get antsy. I found myself sitting there not comfortable in my skin, and not having fun or paying attention to the racing. I just wanted to be home, where I felt safe, not out in public. It was very sad and lonely. I hated the person I was becoming and just wanted to go back to being me, the fun Jen. I missed her desperately.

It wasn't long after the first episode of this, "Anxiety" that I started to notice my world was closing in, and I was having more anxiety issues and symptoms. One day Keith and I, and his family went out to dinner. I remember sitting there just feeling out of it. I sat at the end of the table so if I needed to run to the bathroom because of my symptoms, I had an out. I ordered my dinner, but as soon as it came, I started to notice my breathing was funny, and my heart was beginning to race. I remember thinking, "what the hell is wrong with me? I can't enjoy a dinner out at a restaurant now?! There *has* to be something wrong with me!" And that something wasn't, "anxiety." I ate some of my dinner but moved my plate, so I could put my head down. I just wanted to be out of there. I felt stupid and ashamed. Who the hell puts their head down on a restaurant table that isn't three years old? And why did that make me feel somewhat better? All I know is all of this was fucked up and I felt my life was being stripped of the fun I used to have. Now I couldn't go to dinner, that's one more thing I can scratch from doing. My life was losing the good, and being replaced, in my opinion, with bad and negative experiences.

As my world closed in, I wouldn't drive as much as I used to, I wasn't having any fun, and different and similar symptoms were taking place in my body daily. I was unrecognizable to myself, which wasn't helping my relationship and my lifestyle. I felt empty, but full of fear. I looked at life completely differently, and I hated it. I wished this didn't happen to me. I questioned what I did wrong, I have never smoked, nor done any drugs. I certainly love my cocktails and wine, but to the extent of putting anything else in my body, that was it. I was active, and ate decently, I'm sure that could have been a little better, but seriously, I was running out of things to tell myself because all I thought was, "there is a medical condition wrong with me and I'm going to pass out and die." Period. These were the words that now looped through my mind.

Through all of this I kept remembering who I used to be. The image of my former self was fading. It's like the old me was walking away and my current self was extending a hand to say, "please don't go." As if I did something wrong and my old self was disappearing before my eyes because for some reason, I needed to change and go forth without the old Jen. I wondered if she would remember me as we drifted further apart from another. It was one of the craziest times of my life.

CHAPTER TWO

CHASING ELUSIVE ANSWERS

Living my new lifestyle of fear and loathing was absolutely miserable! I would get up every morning during the week, get ready for work, make my English muffin with peanut butter, get in my car, crack the window for air—because for some reason I felt it made me breathe easier, and drive to my job. I worked at an auto dealer about forty minutes away from home, which happened to be close to my mom's house, thankfully.

At work, I had a desk job, but interreacted with a lot of the dealership. So, when I felt antsy from my funny breathing or body symptoms, I would get up and move.

Unfortunately, during this period of my life and what they labeled my symptoms as, "anxiety" my ass was on the exam table at my doctor's office at least twice a week. On one occasion after an EKG they performed for symptoms of what I called, "a weird heartbeat" the doctors office called and said, "you need to get to this office now, they have found something on the EKG." I must admit I was ecstatic to have found what was going on with me, but that quickly melted into fear of having an actual heart problem. My days would start out with worry of a heart attack or stroke, and whichever one began in the morning, by the afternoon the second one would make its worried appearance.

Once in the doctor's office, they ran another EKG, and then connected me with a cardiologist for my Echo Cardiogram. They were able to get me in quickly, and let me tell you, for someone who fears their heart and heartbeats, this was not the best experience. I sat there and watched the monitor, I could see my heart pumping, I listened to the beats, which I asked if they could silence because it was making me uncomfortable and literally waited for the ahhhhh-haaaaa, there's the problem! On one hand, I was thankful the tech didn't run out of the room for the Doctor, and on the other I was hoping to get something from him just giving me hope that I would be okay, no matter the outcome. I left the appointment feeling like this would be the test and appointment that brought my old self back. See, I *knew* there was a problem... I pushed and pushed for an answer from my team of Doctors and staff, and could pull the, "anxiety" label from my symptoms. The nervousness of waiting for the results the few days after came with a quick phone call with a cheerful technician saying, "your Echo Cardiogram is completely normal, you have a very healthy heart and have nothing to worry about." While I felt elated there was nothing wrong with my heart, I was back to square one with my symptoms and still had this, "anxiety" diagnosis.

As I lived my new life of fear and nervousness, life was still motoring on. Keith and I still were going camping, on dates and to fun places. Unfortunately, I was a train wreck of nerves. I tried not to show it, but I wouldn't have gotten an Oscar for my performance either.

We had a little twenty-foot toy hauler trailer that we purchased together, and one evening we took it to a Casino to a concert. Trace Adkins and Buddy Jewel were playing the Lucky Eagle Casino in Rochester, WA. Being a Country fan, Keith was swaying my music interests toward the Country Radio airwaves and to see Trace would be amazing!

Once we arrived down there, we went into the smoke-filled

casino, ordered a cocktail, and gambled. We then retreated to our trailer to hang out and wait until we went in to eat dinner before the concert. I laid down and tried to relax. I felt my breathing was off, I just kept taking deep, sighing breaths, that annoyingly entertained Keith. He was being goofy and trying to make me laugh, but I was so nervous of why this was happening here. I'm trying to have fun and enjoy this concert and time with him, I wasn't having it. I just sat there annoyed with myself, and now him. I didn't even want to go to the concert.

After I regrouped myself as best as I could, we went in for dinner, and then to the concert. We stood toward the back by an exit. That was planning on my part. It was very crowded, and the venue was dark, but the music was so good! I caught myself acting like the old Jen, having a good time, not worrying, it was a glimpse of what I have been missing. Swaying to the music and singing was taking the worry off my worry. Then it seemed to come to a screeching halt once I realized I wasn't worrying. I can't make this stuff up — I began to worry why I wasn't worried and then the fear set in. I literally felt the fun run out of my body. Before I knew it, I was in my own head trying to figure out why these episodes were happening to me.

I happened to turn to my left as I worried silently, with a smile on my face so I didn't tip off Keith that I was about to lose my freaking mind and to my delight, there were two paramedics standing there. It was like I won the jackpot! Hell yeah! If they see me go down, they will help me. I'm SAFE! I remember thinking, "what the hell?" I'm sitting here about to pass out and die, and now I'm feeling better because I literally have my own set of paramedics right here, instantly, I felt ten times better.

I felt so much better we ordered cocktails and we danced and sang through the rest of the concert.

We walked out to our trailer and unlike before, we laughed and talked about the concert and enjoyed the rest of the evening.

The experience of the paramedics saving my day lingered with me. I went from fear to fun. While there was still some nervousness, it seemed to magically disappear with knowing I was okay and safe with help very close at hand.

I began to wonder what anxiety really was. Because anxiety to me, is just a worry issue. I'm not worrying, I'm having actual body symptoms.

All I know is I wanted a diagnosis because there *is* something wrong with me. This doesn't just happen to a healthy mid-twenty-year-old who now by all accounts has a healthy heart, and to this point, a clean bill of health. Trust me, I have had the blood tests, and more to try to get the diagnosis I have been craving, but I just keep being told you have, "anxiety." Could it really be anxiety? I still couldn't wrap my head around that. But I was beginning to wonder why I was being told this is what I have. So, I started to investigate this label that kept being placed on myself and my symptoms.

Anxiety is defined by Merriam Webster Dictionary as a noun; 1. Apprehensive uneasiness or nervousness usually over an impending or anticipated ill: a state of being anxious.

The second definition of anxiety just about stopped me in my tracks. 2. (medical): an abnormal and overwhelming sense of apprehension and far often marked by physical signs (such as tension, sweating, and increased pulse rate), by doubt concerning the reality and nature of the threat, and by self-doubt about one's capacity to cope with it.

Well damn it, this sounds like they're defining me and my symptoms. I couldn't completely comprehend how my body, well my mind, could be doing this to me. How can a rapid heartbeat, chest pain and fear of a heart attack and/or stroke just come out of nowhere? I certainly have the greatest explanation for my symptoms, but I was perplexed as to how they would just happen? I know our mind is a powerful thing, but I don't know if it is stubbornness, or lack of wanting to believe, in the back of my mind, I felt I'd be missing a major ailment by moving forward with this diagnosis of having anxiety. I mean, come on, anxiety is commonly known as the worry word... not a medical diagnosis. "This makes me anxious." "I have some anxiety about this test coming up." "The weather storm coming in has my dogs anxious." Nobody goes around saying, "My heart just raced, I have this urge to run, I feel my chest getting tight, my breathing has become shallow and my vision is beginning to tunnel and I feel like I'm going to pass out... oh wait, that's just anxiety. I'm okay!" Hell no!! You run because you're grabbing the phone to dial 911 to help you before you die and it's too late! I'll "believe" this anxiety diagnosis to a small degree, because with its definition, it's the closest diagnosis I have had yet, but there *has* to be something more wrong with me, and I can't turn a blind eye to what is happening to me and call it just "anxiety." In the meantime, I spoke with my doctor who was finally happy I listened, and they put me on Paxil Extended Release. I was fearful to take a medication, since well, ya know, I didn't want to purposely take something that would make my body symptoms appear, but I was also drained of worry and fear of them appearing unsuspectingly at any given time. I gave in, and began my prescription, and went on the notion that if this doesn't work, then there is definitely something more wrong with me. Now I wait in my worried little body for what is next.

CHAPTER THREE

_____

A MILLION REASONS TO STAY

I was told that within a couple weeks, that I would notice a difference in my anxiety, basically that I wouldn't be so edgy and nervous all the time. For me, it was almost immediate. I felt like I was smiling more, not worried as much and just all-around vibrating on a level that I was actually, happy. I had forgotten what happy felt like.

While I wasn't too thrilled for being on medication, I was surprised by the results in just a matter of days.

What I noticed in trying to keep this good mood going, I began to do everything the same each day. From getting up and my routine, to making sure my peanut butter English muffin was ready to go with me to work, taking the same route to work and doing the same things once home. I repeated myself daily. It was painstaking to do but living in the hell of worry and fear was far from what I wanted to do. I felt if I did everything correctly each day, I would be rewarded with no episodes of anxiety for the day. If my day went off track, I would feel the fear of anxiety coming over me and then I was watching everything like a hawk.

For the most part, things were settling into the new normal of life post anxiety attacks. I was not the same person anymore, I used to not worry about my health, future, and life, that was then, but with the medication, and even with the lift of worry, the angst of anxiety looming around any corner existed.

I was able to function, so-to-speak, and do the things I enjoyed doing. Keith and I would go out to dinner on Thursdays. There was this one place that made excellent Taco's. The restaurant is on the waterfront, just inside a channel from the Puget Sound. They always had great music, but it wasn't too loud, so we could still carry on a conversation. We began to travel a bit more, too, even though the car/driving fear was present. I believe it was because my first anxiety attack was behind the wheel.

We liked to camp, ride quads, travel to Portland, Oregon and stay in nice hotels, head to Eastern Washington—you name it. Anything that had to do with Washington and Oregon, we liked to explore. However, there was this one stretch of road that would send me into worry and anxiety prior to even hitting the highway. It was Highway 6 in Oregon. This highway connected the coast to the outer veins of Portland, and it was long, windy, one lane, and had no cell service one you traveled a couple miles in on the Highway. It was always the last part of our trip to the dunes outside Tillamook, Oregon, and the first part as we headed East towards home. I don't know what was worse; getting in the truck and knowing it was coming or being there all weekend knowing what was coming once we started heading home. Either way, it wasn't my favorite road. It took about fifty minutes to travel the highway and even though we crossed this pass often, I never paid attention to the landmarks, such as restaurants, gas stations, parks or turn outs that would make me think, "okay, we are near being off this road." That's how much fear this road brought to my being introverted in worry about my health and some health issue that would just so happen on this road, because damn it, that's how bad my luck was! And did I mention there was no cell phone service?

I was always so hopeful for that sigh of relief, the one that says, "yes, it's over, nothing happened. Now you can have fun!" I always received it, but I was always in fear that feeling would fail me one day. So, I just worried in case, because I felt if I didn't worry once, that is when it would happen, and I would be blindsided. Seriously—this anxiety fear bs crippled and mind-tripped my life. But I wasn't going to worry about not worrying. It was just safer to worry a little bit and deal with it.

That being said. If I worried a little, stuck to my daily routine and took my medication, I would be granted a decent day. The dark cloud of fear and anxiety seemed to be lifting, but I respected the terror and horror of what it meant in my life. I began to get angry at what my life has become. I questioned why I just couldn't be normal like I was before. "What did I do to deserve this?" would loop in my mind as I would reminisce and miss my old life. I felt I became unrecognizable to myself, and obviously Keith now sees this change and while it's difficult for him, he feels bad for me and he too, misses how I used to be.

Anxiety isn't just crippling to the person it has its grips on, it changes the whole landscape of a life, the life the anxious has around them, and the future of what is yet to come. The present becomes the worry of the future, and the past becomes envied by the sufferer. Trust me. Still to this day, I felt after my first anxiety/panic attack, that I lost the original Jennifer. I was banned from being the me I've always known, but to look back now, I did worry and had fears. I just didn't know why or what it was.

When I was in grade school, I walked home from school, about six blocks. Which in itself blows my mind because for one, I would not let my children do that at all, I watch my daughter go to the mailbox right outside our home for goodness sakes! But two, I wouldn't walk the same six blocks I did in school as an adult! I was brave and independent I suppose.

I remember walking home one day, I was about two blocks from our apartment building, and I happened to notice this one car drive by me. The road beside me was a four lane, thirty-five mile per hour main drag that connected our little Kent, Washington's downtown to the houses, warehouses, and freeways.

This car had kids in the back seat, and I kid you not, I *swore* I saw my little twin brother in the back seat. This kid locked eyes with me and suddenly there was this shear panic of, "someone took my little brother!" I started running as fast as I could home. I bolted through the door like a freight train with near tears as I just knew that was my brother and I would never see him again. Well, there he was sitting on the floor with his twin brother playing. I was so relieved and thrilled to see him. I gave him a kiss and literally played off the fear with my mom. I know that there was a reason to be fearful, but I went over the top! I internalized this thought and now I was sensitive to their safety and care. Because now, "what if" my brothers were kidnapped, or lost, I'd lose my mind and be so upset. From that point on, I worried about my brothers. Actually, I obsessed with worry about my brothers! This time, my mom was aware that I had something going on.

Each Christmas, my entire extended family would get together and celebrate. My aunt usually hosted, and she lived in a big neighborhood that always boosted lots of decorated houses to ooohh and ahhh over. There was a decision to go for a walk after dinner before we opened presents and had dessert. I was excited until my uncle said that my brothers can stay back and play with their toys. Uh what? I began to find a reason to excuse myself from the walk. I worried that my brothers could worry that my mom left and leave the house to go find her and get lost. Oh, my goodness, I was shaking with fear. I made it out the front door and positioned myself near the cut glass window to look inside to make sure my brothers were safe and not trying to come. My mom leaned over and said, "stop worrying, they are fine!" Now she knows. She sees my fear obsession with their safety.

We went for a walk, took in all the lights, well, the best I could, and as we neared the house, I began to have fun again. I walked inside to see my brothers safely playing with their toys and getting excited to open gifts!

This one fear shaped me into the mom that I am today. Little did

I know that while I felt I missed the normal Jennifer, there was so much more I didn't recognize about myself until I had shifted to the anxious side. Yes, I worried — a lot! I had uncontrolled thoughts and fears, but they grew upon themselves until my mind gave into the fear of the thoughts and my body began to mimic symptoms I was creating in my head.

CHAPTER FOUR

THE BIRTH OF MOMXIETY

"God Gave me you for the ups and downs.
God gave me you for the day of doubt."
-Blake Shelton

As life churned each day, I was making strides in recovering from anxiety and panic disorder. While I did have some episodes, they weren't nearly as bad as they used to be. Keith and I were now engaged to be married—we wanted a fun, Vegas style wedding so we could vacation, too. Of course, we would drive, since I'm afraid of flying, and why would I put a fear into my life since I was keeping fear *out* of my life.

I was taking my medication daily, there was no increase in dosage, but I was trying to find a way to cope without my anxiety medication. Having anxiety has gifted me with the fear of medication now. I have stopped taking all cold medications, including even Tylenol. This decision was made after I had taken an Expectorant cough syrup. I felt like I was hyper, and my heart was racing like crazy. I felt out of control and in that moment, I added all medicine to the, "do not do" list that I've created in my head. It's been nearly fifteen years ago since I've had any medication as I write this book.

My fiancé and I were living together by now and wanted to move to a house that had a bit more space and a bigger garage. We are ATV riders, and Keith has a big collection that seemed to grow each season. We found a house that was a little bit out of town, near a lake. You could see the lake from our laundry room area, on your tippy toes, if you leaned to the right. We found that to be a win of a lake view.

We packed up our old house and moved into the new one with the help of his Uncle Pat, but I wasn't feeling my best. Actually, feeling sick to my stomach. I think it was nerves from moving and being a little out of my element in routine and I'm sure somewhere along the way, with eating out due to packing, it was catching up to me. However, there was this little inkling to get a pregnancy test. So, I did.

As I took the test in our new house, I popped it into the cabinet and went to find Keith to see what the dinner plan was. We decided on Mexican food, and even though I felt bad, food sounded so good, too! We also told Uncle Pat we'd take him for all his help with our move.

I checked into the test and was shocked! I was pregnant. According to this stick, at least. I didn't say a word to Keith, as I wanted to share with him in private, but he sure found out something was up when we ordered margaritas at the Mexican Restaurant. Keith and Uncle Pat put their order in, and I said make mine a virgin and I swear Keith's head shot over to me with rapid speed, nothing I have ever seen before.

With a "what the hell" worded to me in silence with his mouth, I just shook my head and said, yep.

We both were shocked, a little upset for a second, and then happy to know our family was growing. Our idea of a Vegas wedding was now off the table. Instead, we found a quaint church near our home and went on the Dinner train that wound its way to Woodinville, WA and the wine country as our reception. Little did we know, when we booked an entire car on the train and family and friends came to fill it on our reception, that we were starting a yearly tradition of booking the car and enjoying our anniversary with them all year after year. Until it closed due to a highway being widened and the tracks being removed. It was a sad, sad last trip that year and each August, we still miss it.

With family and friends aware of our bundle of joy, I was aware and concerned about taking my anxiety medication while being pregnant. I know side effects are there for me, but what about birth defects? What about chemical changes for both of us? Well this just started a whole new level of worry, and it didn't just include me. Now I worried about my unborn child. The "what if" of his or her wellbeing and what I was potentially doing was now a forefront worry and calling my doctor to discuss this was top priority.

My doctor explained there shouldn't be any worry but being a worrier and a great investigator with words and symptoms, "shouldn't be," means there could be, and I wasn't okay with taking the medication. While I was terrified about losing something that helped in my daily anxiety and would be panic attacks, that I feel have been diminished due to this medication, the fear of doing damage to our unborn child scared me even more. So, it was time to ween myself off this medication, which was an anxiety in and of its own. My dosage was cut way down, went to every other day, to every second, third, etc. until I was not taking it anymore. I had major dizzy spells, which for an anxious person is just agonizing. I went through the, "what is wrong with me" and the "why am I feeling this way?" to "what if I am having a stroke" and finally, "what if pass out" because I felt so light-headed and sick. However, knowing I was doing this for the greater good of our child, and relating my symptoms to knowing this is coming off medication allowed me some relief and self-talk to not send me over the edge. There was something about knowing that direct relation to something that made a huge difference in my life. All the other times I would have similar symptoms, I had no idea where they came from. I was living a normal-ish life one minute and running scared for my life the next because of physical symptoms, which had no relation to anything other than the sudden onset of symptoms.

Thankfully, I also had something else to distract me from being off my medication completely, we were having a girl! Oh, and I loved to eat. A lot!! I think I traded in my fears of anxiety to making sure I had two lunches. Oh, and my cravings of citrus were out of control! I craved lemonade and orange soda like it was going to go out of style. I loved macaroni and cheese, Mexican food — especially enchiladas and don't get me started on the Baja Bowl at Taco Del Mar. Unreal was the deliciousness stuffed into the bowl topped with sour cream and guacamole. My mouth may be watering as I type this book out. But in all seriousness, post anxiety medication and detoxing from that, life seemed to be exciting and fun again! I was due in December, the 26th to be exact, and with the holidays coming up, it's my favorite time of the year. I was feeling excitement, but a little nervousness for the delivery of our daughter. Yes, this mom was already visualizing and internalizing the delivery. The momxiety has already begun, because it's not just my anxiety anymore, it was the anxiety surrounding a little human, her delivery, her success and her growing up. It's a level of anxiety I didn't know existed until I became pregnant. The worry of myself was definitely there and present, it was somewhat controlled at the moment, for reasons other than it's been a distraction being pregnant, and the wedding, the holidays, and her arrival.

Maybe I have begun to relax and live the life I am supposed to be living, mostly anxiety and panic disorder free. It was a thought that I toyed with, but not lightly. I surely didn't want to wake the beast of anxiety within if I thought positive for too long. Yes—this was actually a fear of mine. What I had dealt with to this point in my life was no joke. An anxiety and panic disorder are life crippling, life changing, and for me, felt like a life sentence. However, still taking one day, and one worry at a time, I was keeping the new, "momxiety" at bay, at least until the next episode.

CHAPTER FIVE

———————

ME, MYSELF AND ANXIETY

I'm not one to sit around, and have others do things for me, so when I couldn't bend over to tie my shoes because my belly was so big, I bought slip on sneakers. And when I decided to host Thanksgiving dinner at our home, at nearly eight months pregnant, telling me no wasn't going to stop me either.

I had never cooked a Turkey, and have always wanted to hang around the house, watch the Macy's Thanksgiving Day Parade on TV, cook and being lazy in comfy clothes and slippers. Looking back, I think I was wanting to start our own family traditions in our home, and invite our family over to join us, so why not start being big and pregnant with our first child?

The dinner was a complete success, and what was even more impressive were my swollen ankles. I knew your feet could swell, but holy moly! They were like quadruple the size! I was told to lay down with my feet up, so I did for a bit. My mom and Keith were cleaning up dinner in the kitchen and I felt bad they were having to do so, so I got up. Only to be scolded to sit down. My words were nicer than theirs in how I was told to sit and relax. They were right, but it wasn't easy, that's for sure.

From the Thanksgiving festivities and the blooming ankles, we, and I mean, my husband, said we're not going to fully decorate for Christmas, and we will go to Christmas dinner, not host ourselves. I was so sad, but I knew he was right. I go ALLLL out at Christmas, the tree, and every surface in our home has something on it. It usually takes me a full day to get it done, and our house was only 800 square feet, so imagine the décor if you will. So, I reluctantly agreed, but definitely didn't like it one bit.

Just before Christmas, the home we rented had a plumbing issue, and the owners had sent out a great guy who owned a local plumbing business to repair the problem. During the day, I had noticed I was having some tightening and discomfort every so often in my stomach. While we were a few weeks away from delivery, I began to get anxious that something bad was happening. Yes, it's always the negative thought before the positive. I called my doctor, who asked me to keep track of how often this was happening and to call back if there was a clear pattern, otherwise, it was mildly prescribed that I was having Braxton hicks' contractions. Normal, but I worried something could be wrong with me and possibly our daughter. My anxiety spiked, and I began to get hot and have an increased heart rate.

Rod, the plumber of At Your Service Plumbing, arrived to a very pregnant woman and a husband with a notepad and pen. His very first concern was if I was okay, and if he could help in any way. I believe for an instant we all had an image of Rod rushing us to the hospital in his work van, surrounded by pipes, fittings, and ground covers.

Rod went to work, and Keith kept on taking notes for my contractions. Every so often Rod would check in, and verify I was okay and comfortable. While there was some pain associated with the contractions, for the most part I was in good spirits, and trying to focus on the positive and not dive into the negative mindset that I knew quite well.

The plumbing issue was fixed, and Rod made sure of my comfort before he left. We were so thankful for him and his concern, that we began being their customer for that simple reason, plus he did a great job on our plumbing. I love kind and considerate people. He brought an ease to a semi stressful situation and I will never forget that. (Sadly, Rod lost his brief battle with mesothelioma on July 1, 2010. One hell of a man we still miss.)

I called our doctor to let him know the contractions were irregular and slowing for the evening. Which made me happy, but also anxious for what was to come. I'm kind of a wuss for pain, so if this was bothering me, I'm not sure what to think of with the real pain of childbirth. Yes, I know there's drugs that can be administered, but I'm fearful of medication. It was an odd place to be in because I knew pain was on the agenda for childbirth, but taking a medication I have never had, made for a highly anxious and emotional state of being. I couldn't go back, I had to give birth. Trust me, the thought was there for a Nano second. This anxiety was simmering to a boil and I knew at a rapid speed, a panic attack was looming. I relaxed as best as I could, and when I felt it wasn't working, I got up and walked around, which helped calm everything down. So much that I was able to sleep that evening.

With Christmas approaching, I put up my six-foot lighted, faux tree garland around our arched door opening and hung a few decorations from it. This was *not* my idea of decorating. Yes, I was being a baby, but I really wanted a tree. I thought for sure I'd be able to convince him by now, but my efforts were denied and while I still reluctantly agreed, I wished for a tree. I thought a sweet picture of our daughter under our tree would make for a cute photo opportunity. I don't think holding her up under a funky, out of shape lighted garland around the doorway was practical. And in case you're wondering, I'm still bitter over no tree, but I showed my husband. We have at least six trees up in our home each Christmas. I think no tree that year changed me, lol.

We were on weekly visits to the doctor's office at this point, with being one week plus a couple days out from our due date, we were nearing the meeting of our daughter, and my anxiety of delivery.

Our doctor's appointment was scheduled for Monday, December 20, 2004. Ironically, just a night or two before this appointment, I was woken up from a deep sleep with what felt like an acrobat in my stomach. She was definitely moving and making her presence known. I remember grabbing my stomach and sitting up with intent fear that something bad was happening. It just didn't feel right and I sat there in the dark listening and feeling the movements. I woke Keith up and he said it was probably gas. Why do men always think that? It was one big movement, and then just the kicks and flutters, so I relaxed back to laying down, and just laid there until I fell asleep, but felt I slept with one eye open just in case.

It wasn't until my doctor's appointment that I knew exactly what had gone on. I loved our Doctor; his name was Dr. Bruce Romig and he was absolutely the *best* doctor! His sense of humor was awesome, and I explained to him what happened that one night, his answer was priceless.

He asked me to lay down, so he can check the size of my stomach and her placement and said, "well, these are the wrong cheeks down here." I said, "what?" He said your baby is now breech, what you felt was her flipping that night. WHATTTTT?? I said, "what do we do with that?" with intense fear inside. He said, "we could numb you and manually flip her, which would leave nail imprints on your stomach, and not feeling the best, or do a c-section." You've got to be kidding me.

Suddenly, I was stricken with fear and a decision that had to be decided right then. I definitely didn't want to manually flip her but now I was faced with a major surgery that I would be awake for! Dr. Romig left the room briefly so we could decide. He came back in and said that I can fit you in tomorrow morning for the c-section if you go that route. You have *no* idea how panicked I was in this moment. I felt out of control, I felt sick and knew that I was going into surgery tomorrow. I agreed to the "fitting in of a c-section" delivery and was given instructions to not eat after midnight and be at the hospital bright and early.

I was in a state of shock and full on momxiety mode. I was going in for surgery, tomorrow. I was giving birth, tomorrow. I was doing something I have never done in my life, two at one time. I was a train wreck of anxiety, nerves, and anticipation. Inside I was trying not to scare myself even more. After all, a major surgery is scary. While I know Dr. Romig has the expertise and I know for certain I was in great hands, I was still scared out of my skin. I worried about how this would be for our daughter, too. And why the heck did she have to flip and go breech on me? If there was any sort of a win, per se, in my court it was I didn't have to endure the pain and anxiety of childbirth. Yes, I'd have recovery to deal with, I didn't have to push a baby out and in some weird, twisted way, that made me feel better.

Keith and I began to call our families and our friends and share the news of our daughter's arrival the next day. I called my mom and she said, don't you worry, I will be at the hospital in the morning! I asked if she would be in the operating room with me, and she assured me she would. Keith's mom and dad would be there, too. And I asked if his mom would be there in the OR as well. Unfortunately, due to their regulations, I could only have two people in there with me. I felt horrible to let Keith's mom know I chose my mom, but she tearfully understood. I wish it could have been different.

That night I slept well. Why? I have no idea to this day. I think I wore myself out with my anxious thoughts and the edgy, high vibration of nervousness I was dealing with. I was scared but felt a level of comfort at the same time. Maybe it was because for the last time, my husband and I would be alone in our house together. Keith was very strong and knew my fight of anxiety, depression, and panic, and did all he could to assure me, and maybe some of that crept in and I heard it and listened to him.

Nevertheless, it was the eve of life changing moments for us, and we kissed each other good night, said we loved each other and fell asleep quickly.

CHAPTER SIX

ANXIETY TRIP

As night gave way to morning on this First Day of Winter, we awoke to an early alarm to get the day moving. Oddly enough for me, I was nervous, but not in my normal, anxious, shaking, "what is wrong with me" way. I have noticed this before. One-time Keith and I flew to Las Vegas for his mom's 50th birthday, I worried like crazy once we booked our tickets, I had the, "what if's" firing off like no tomorrow. But once I got to the airport and went through the motions, and got on the plane, I was somewhat okay. While I was nervous in the air, and had to relax myself constantly, I was doing it. I will say that I did think of the worst-case scenarios and played them out rather dramatically in my head—sometimes I wonder if I could be a horror story writer the way my mind travels in thought. However, that was the last time I flew, and it was 2003.

We quickly got ready and grabbed our hospital bag and began our road trip to Labor and Delivery. We stopped and picked Keith's mom up on our way. I believe she was more nervous than me that morning. It wasn't a long distance from her home to the hospital, and once we arrived, my mom was waiting for me inside the Birthing Suites waiting room.

The waiting room was decorated with pink and blue stockings, and a big fancy tree with pink, blue, and white ornaments, a nice warm touch to having a baby at Christmas time. I checked in, and then was wheeled down the hall to the Surgery prep area. Now this is getting real, and fast!

The warm, Christmas like waiting room where I just was, now gave way to an assembly line of moms-to-be, waiting for their c-section. Don't get me wrong, this is a nice hospital, but having a c-section doesn't come with the nice birthing suites in the soft lighting, and relaxing furniture. Instead I had a curtained off section with the blue-gray walls, a TV that didn't have a chance at capturing my attention, and the action of nurses getting everyone ready, in a speed of urgency.

Keith, my mom; Roberta, and his mom; Karen, stood around me as I gowned up and got into bed. I was immediately given an IV and since Dr. Romig was doing his job so well, my time was moved up, which meant I had to be given IV and meds much faster. So much faster that when the nurse turned up the IV to get fluids in me faster, I felt super light-headed and saw stars! Yep, I was going to pass out! She assured me I was fine, just to relax and calm down if I could. Well, sister, you don't know me, and those words don't do a damn thing! Thankfully that situation was short lived, and I didn't pass out. I just sat there in a constant state of worry because I felt off and that led to an increased level of anxiety coursing through my veins.

It began to get real when they came into pre-op to get the mom next to me. I was next. I knew surgery was coming but knowing it would be my turn in a bit was very unnerving and I began to really struggle with my anxiety. My breathing felt labored, the big deep breaths were drawing my attention, which was a sign for me that I am approaching a full-on panic attack. I was hooked up to heart monitors, IV's and more, so the beeping and visuals of what was happening inside me definitely did not help. I was trying to keep it to myself, but my mom reached over at one point and just rubbed my arm and said I would be just fine. Sometimes a mom's touch can rest things, which did help, but it didn't clear the fog of anxiety out fully.

I knew my operating room time was coming as the nurses started to converge around me. Keith and my mom were asked to get into their scrubs, I was given a stomach neutralizer and a little run down of the events that were about to take place. I would be going into the operating room by myself, I'd be given the spinal and then Keith and my mom could come in. Easy, I said to myself.

It was my turn. Oh, the sudden onset of nerves made my legs feel like Jell-O! The nurses came in to get me in their full scrubs, it was the point of no return now. I kissed Keith and my mom and reluctantly walked with the nurses, all the while holding the back of my gown, down the hall into the Operating Room.

I first noticed how freezing cold the OR was, I was already shaking with my nerves, this was artic cold to me. I was walked over to the table and helped up. The nurses were so wonderful and assured me I would be just fine. By this point I had told them I was so nervous and scared, I couldn't help it. They asked me questions about who would be coming to see me after the birth, and what I would eat once I left the hospital. Questions that helped to direct me back from my anxious mindset.

The anesthesiologist would also be right by my side, well my head to be exact, as he introduced himself and what his role was in this process. He was in charge of making sure I didn't feel a thing. He became my favorite person.

It was time for the spinal, and I have always heard you never want to see the needle. Well, folks, this is very, very true statement. I was given a pillow, and a sweet nurse stood in front of me as my feet hung off the Operating room table and she pulled me toward her, exposing the round of my back. She rubbed my shoulders and quietly talked to me. The anesthesiologist gave his step by step directions, which included deep breaths and holding my breath. As I felt only a small pinch at first, I began to just feel calm, for some weird reason.

Then it was the big needle time, and yes—it IS big! He said this would sting a little and at that exact moment, there was a sting, then a warmth that took over my entire body. I couldn't move my legs, feel my legs or anything below my chest. I began to panic a little! Then everything started to happen fast! I was laid down, positioned, a curtain went up by my chest, to hide whatever was happening further south, and Keith and my mom were let in and then suddenly, I couldn't feel my tongue. Oh my God!! I can't feel my tongue! I called out to the anesthesiologist, who was on the phone, and said something is wrong, "I can't feel my tongue." He said, "you are fine, I'm monitoring your vitals and there's nothing wrong, you just have a high spinal." Well, by the time my mom and Keith walked over, I was biting onto my tongue, because I feared I would swallow it because I couldn't feel it, and it would cut off my breathing and then I'd die on the OR table. Yep, full on panic attack as I laid there virtually paralyzed from the tongue down. I felt the pulling and tugging from my stomach area, I was still biting my tongue, but was noticing it wasn't as dire to do so. Who knows, maybe the anthologist slipped something to relax me into the IV. Even though I was fearful of medication, at that moment, I could have used something to calm me down.

Then I heard her cry. She is here! Finally!! I did it! Suddenly, the anxiety and miserable, negative thoughts were gone. In an instant! She had strong lungs as she cried and shivered from the cold operating room. Miss Kyla Jean Westby was born on Tuesday, December 21st, 2004 at 10:38am, weighing seven pounds, five ounces and nineteen inches long. She was wrapped up quickly and handed over to Keith to meet his little girl, then Keith brought her over to me. I couldn't do much other than kiss her on the cheek as I was strapped down on the Operating table, still. It was a quick meeting as Keith and Kyla went with the nurse to give her a bath and get her ready to show off to our waiting family and friends! My mom stayed back with me, and we chatted and laughed as Dr. Romig sewed me back up. She was making fun of me for biting onto my tongue when she walked in. By this point I could see the humor in the situation, but man it was very scary for a second. It would be something I didn't live down for a long time. Ah, what anxiety makes you do.

I relaxed for a short time in recovery and then brought to my family suite. The warmth of the lights and comfortable setting allowed me to relax and take in the birth of Kyla. We had a constant flow of visitors, family and friends brought flowers and cards to show their love for us and our daughter. It was a beautiful time.

Our team of nurses were the best. We were very well taken care of and having to stay two nights in the hospital due to a c-section, I sure wasn't minding that one bit. There was one thing missing, I noticed I had no anxiety. Like none. I wasn't concerned of something bad going on with me, and I certainly didn't have any symptoms. The only thing that was bothering me was the pain relief! The morphine made my face itch like my skin was crawling with bugs, and the nausea that accompanied it was not okay. I was moved to another pain medication, but it had to be orally taken and it wasn't too long that I found out that my clock in my suite was not on time with the rest of the hospital. It took two rounds of medication for the nurse to run in and apologize to me with a cup of pills after being off the pain meds for two hours because of the discrepancy. I was never as happy to see a nurse as I was in that moment.

The hospital stay was just what I needed. It was an anxious trip of emotions, symptoms, and fear to get here, and have our daughter. Everything I feared was a distant memory, but I was happy I feared it, because I overcame the fears and proved them and myself, in a way, wrong. Was this a time of change for me? Was I really over-coming this anxiety and panic disorder that has crippled my life? The fears that have stolen life changing moments that should be exciting ones, but instead have been packed with fear. It sure felt like some-thing clicked and changed for the better. I was (dare I say it) happy and feeling free of the negativity. I was enjoying the sounds of our daughter, changing diapers, and the warm cuddles she so lovingly snuggled into. I decided to not dwell on why something was different, but for probably the first time since all this anxiety found its way into my life, I chose to be happy and enjoy the moment. And it was one of the best moments in my life.

CHAPTER SEVEN

WRECKING BALL

We were released from the hospital just two days before Christmas. We received our sweetest gift early and were eager to bring her home and celebrate the Holiday with family and friends.

Keith took a week off, and I was so thankful for that. We could all get settled into our routines and comforts before things truly got back to a normal pace. All, meaning me, because I'm nowhere near a routine person. I take each day as it comes. It drives Keith crazy; I might add.

With no tree in our home, just a sad looking piece of fake garland with lights, I took my shot at getting a sleeping Santa picture with our newborn at the mall. It was quickly decided that was not the best idea to bring a two-day old into the mall with germs and illnesses. While I understood, I was sad to not capture a sweet precious picture that could be treasured for our lifetime.

We anticipated being up several times during the night, so Keith and I got a game plan together. We both would get up, changer her, feed her and rock her to sleep. With a high five right before we said good night — we were ready.

Well, our little bundle of joy decided she would just sleep

through the night! She literally woke up at 5am! I flew out of bed at one point during the night in a panic because I thought something was wrong! She couldn't be sleeping through the night already? And trust me, the momxiety of SIDS was alive and well in my thought process in just two days of her birth!

The time Keith was home allowed me to get comfortable with being back home, rest with the recovery of my c-section and adjust to life with a newborn. It seemed almost effortless, which led me to believe that there was something lurking around the corner. What I mean by lurking, is my anxiety. I felt things were going to well. Isn't it crazy how you can worry about something bad happening, at the same time worry that it's going way to good? Yes—this is how I rolled, and it was mind-twisting.

We had a steady flow of visitors the first week, and Kyla slept through most of it. She liked her sleep, and her independence. We loved the swaddle blanket idea, but she did not. She was much happier being in a sleeper with her hands above her head. She cuddled, but on her own time, otherwise, let her lay and have her space.

As the days went by, and Keith was to be going back to work, I began to get anxious. That lurking I was feeling was anticipation of him going back to work, and me doing this on my own. It was going great, but that is because I have him home with me, I felt good, confident, safe, secure, but it was fading off to feeling uneasy, insecure, and unsafe. I knew these feelings all too well.

The night before Keith went back, he was getting ready for bed, at his early bedtime. Something we haven't done for a bit of time. We would stay up and watch TV and hung out, it was so comforting. I immediately didn't like it at all. I was feeling abandoned. Yes, I know he would be in the other room, but he wasn't awake with me, keeping me occupied. Selfish, I know.

I started to feel that anxious buzz in my body. I was trying to not cry, or show I didn't like it, but it suddenly came flooding out. I held our sleeping daughter and just lost it. I was crying so hard I couldn't see and shaking so bad that I had to put her down. Keith questioned me on where this all came from and I said I didn't know; I just didn't want him to go back to work and pleaded for him to stay home one more day. But that wasn't an option, which made my world of hurt even more painful.

He stayed up a little longer and settled me down, but for some reason I couldn't relax in my ability to do this on my own while he's at work. Before it was just me to worry about, and I could barely do that okay with all my anxiety and panic going on, now I have a baby to take into consideration, and that whole idea sent me right back into the misery of being uneasy and tense. Anxiety seems to have found me again.

Thankfully, Keith worked close, and I had neighbors' home around me during the day—a sweet older lady, and her awesome daughter, Ruby and Glenda. Plus, the fire department was just blocks away, too. So, I took some comfort in knowing that I had some safety and security around me.

The mornings were always the most anxious. It was the furthest time Keith was away from home. I would get up, get a bottle for Kyla, turn on the news and veg on the couch. As the morning turned into mid-day, I would put Kyla down for a nap, get dressed and straighten up the house. By this point my anxiety has simmered down a little because I feel I have gone through the toughest part of my day, morning. By four in the afternoon, I would begin the transition of Keith coming home, and I would get excited. I'd make sure the house was completely clean, I would start dinner and light some candles in the house for a welcoming homecoming. He'd get home and my anxiety would disappear for a couple of hours. Every day I did this. It was my vicious circle, but also my vice.

It wasn't too long before I had full blown panic attack, this time as a mom. I was holding Kyla on our loveseat and suddenly I had this hot flash of fear roll over me, my heart began to pound, I couldn't breath and I felt like I was going to pass out. I stood up, ran Kyla over to Keith, grabbed my cordless phone from the kitchen and took off outside my front door and called 911. I didn't allow time for Keith to even ask what was going on, I was in a doom of fear that I was losing my life and I would be leaving Keith and now my daughter alone. I was scared to my core.

By the time the ambulance showed up, I was coming down off this body symptom attack and got the once over, and a "hey, how are you doing, haven't been here for a bit of time, smile and laugh" from the fire department, which are still my favorite people who always made me feel better and safe.

After they left, Keith and I talked, and he asked me about how this suddenly happens. It was a million-dollar question I wish I had the right answer to. It was a constant search to the answer, "why?" that haunted me. I tried to explain the onset of symptoms and it was hard to. I could only tell him that it literally comes with no warning other than I have this urge to run for help and safety because I feel like I'm just going to pass out and die.

For someone who hasn't had the pleasure of these awesome panic attacks, it's a completely foreign language with no interpreter for them to understand. It is not like you can make someone have a panic attack to show them, at times, I wish I could, so he could help me. Maybe I was missing something?

I know it wasn't easy for Keith to see this person he fell in love with look like they are literally losing their minds, running out of the house with 911 on the line and running away from him, because he's not good enough to help me. In all accounts, I felt like I was losing myself, my husband, my daughter, my lifestyle, and my comfort of being alive. I feared death, but I also feared being alive because of what was happening to me.

I feared Keith leaving, too. I felt he had every right to, but I certainly didn't want him to. This thought began a new worry in my life. I felt I needed to be back to the, "normal Jen he met" not the crazy, "this is not the Jen I fell in love with" girl, which fueled my anxiety. It was a daily struggle to be the person I used to be for him, but inside I wasn't, and it was beginning to take its toll.

It seemed easy, just to be me. How I used to be. Have you ever tried to be the person you used to be? I know who I am, but who was I? What did I like? What did I do? What did I act like? How did I love him? Suddenly, the appearance of not knowing who I was, and could I pass it off like I do know was agonizing and strenuous.

It felt the more I tried to be the old me, it was backfiring at rapid speed. I was so strung out on anxiety and panic, that with each worry, I lost the image or memory of the person I once was. It made me fear I would never be the person I used to be, and I have completely lost my grasp on ever being that person again. Which to me, led me to believe Keith couldn't fall in love with me in this new normal, because hell, I couldn't even fall in love with myself. I hated myself, I hated my life, I hated that this was happening to me, I hated I couldn't be the person I know, well, once knew. So, how could he?

To top it off, I'm a mom and that has changed me as a person, too. After having the panic attack where I left the house and gave Kyla to Keith, it set in my mind that, "what if I'm alone and this happens again? What would I do with Kyla?" Talk about a surgency of anxiety and total panic of passing out with my daughter at home alone, well, the fears doubled and tripled in size, and from that point on, it was full Momxiety and panic for me.

CHAPTER EIGHT

NOTHING IS SAFE FROM WORRY

I have to say, momxiety and panic can make you do and think some truly strange and unimaginable things. After the first post-delivery attack where I dropped Kyla in Keith's lap and bolted from the house, there was not one day a worry or fear didn't cross my mind.

I got to the point where I didn't want to be home. Which was very strange, because home was, "safe" to me. But the last attack made me concerned of being home alone with Kyla. If I were at a grocery store and this happened, at least I could get help, but then the fear of someone taking my daughter if I passed out scared me, too. This momxiety has brought this game to a whole new level!

I tried to make my outings in the late morning, early afternoon, before nap time. It allowed me to get through my morning anxiety but let up some, so I could get out and not be home alone for too long. We would stop by Keith's work and hang out, we'd go to the grocery store—a lot, and shop at the mall. That stroller sure got a lot of miles tacked on thanks to my momxiety.

I had a sudden fear to not give my daughter a bath while I was alone. I worried of sudden body symptoms coming on if she were in the tub, she could drown. These were my struggles and they were certainly real.

I checked on her when she slept, all the time. One night I awoke out of a deep sleep to a fear of her not breathing. I jumped up and went to the bassinet and thought I couldn't see her chest rising and falling, so I moved her, and she woke up, and she wasn't too happy with me, either. I didn't care, I felt a rapid ease of anxiety with her being awake.

The experts, along with friends and family always give you the advice to nap when your baby naps. Not for me! My fear was what if I don't wake up? What if she is lying there all by herself and I'm gone? What would happen? Would she be scared? How long until someone found us? The fear was so real, that even though I was exhausted, I was hell bent to not take a nap in case something bad were to happen.

Not to mention driving still being an issue, while it bothered me, I knew being in public was part of my daily routine now, and driving was needed to get me there. As long as it was in town, I was okay, well sort of. There was a grocery store about a mile away, and there were days I couldn't even drive that distance. My worry about driving with Kyla was, "what if," I pass out while driving and we crash. I couldn't bring myself to the notion that I could hurt my baby by driving my car and this happening. The level of worry would change depending where I went. If it was close, I was okay, a little further out, like Keith's parents, my anxiety would increase. I would take certain roads that drove me past fire stations, or close ones to it in case I needed to call them. I paid attention to road signs, where before an example for my directions were take a right at the blue house and go past the 7-11 and turn left at the house with the green old car that never moves. I hardly relied on street signs to give any sort of directions.

I'd be a hot mess in the car on the way there, but once I arrived, I would settle down and when it was time to drive back, I would be a little more at ease knowing I was going home to my, "safe" place.

I tried to make all my stops, such as a post office drop off, a quick stop to get milk and formula, on my way home from my destination. I felt calmer, because I knew I was going home. I tried this before going places and my body would buzz with nervousness so to me it wasn't worth the extra anxiety, so I changed my routines to stopping on my way home.

If I were to travel to my mom's house, well, that was a completely different story. She was forty-five minutes away, and that was by freeways. Back streets were a lot longer. For a period of time, I would drive the back roads because I felt there was a better chance of pulling over if I needed help, and more places that offered more people in case I needed someone fast. But it took a long time and the anxiety of it taking too long, gave way to me driving the freeways after some time. I think it is interesting how the mind can be satisfied on one thing for so long, then it becomes off limits because the anxiety attaches itself to it. And for me, once that happens, I don't usually go that way or do that thing again.

Once I began driving the freeways, I took note of the three hospitals that were between my mom and our home. There is the hospital in Puyallup, just after I get on the freeway, there's a hospital in Auburn, which was a little more than halfway to my mom's and then there was the hospital in Renton where my mom happened to live right across the street from! I always felt comfortable at her place for some reason.

I also developed a fear of eating at home alone. My momxiety mind would travel to, "What if I choked?" What would happen to me? To Kyla? We would be eating together and what if I passed out from chocking, would she start to choke, too? I turned to soft things and if I did eat a regular breakfast or lunch, I chewed the hell out of my food, kept the phone nearby and a glass of water.

As Kyla grew and her palette was expanding, I worried about allergies and severe ones that could cause her throat to close and she could die. I worried so much, that I quit eating shellfish and peanut butter myself. Two things I absolutely loved. I didn't want to accidently introduce her to them and have a bad reaction take place. I also feared honey, because that is not good for babies under one-year-old. So, no more peanut butter and honey sandwiches. It was a sad day for me. But out of safety and security of her wellbeing, I was not going to put anything that can harm me or my daughter.

The worry of Keith's safety found its way into my life. I would worry about him driving to work and home. Yes, the drive wasn't far, but I would worry the second he hung up the phone when he left work, until I could hear our diesel Ford coming from down the street. It was a reversal of worry in the mornings. I couldn't bear the thought of my doing this parenting thing on my own if something were to happen, so I would just worry, because again, if I didn't, well, I didn't want to take that chance.

Life as a person and a mom, thanks to momxiety, was taking its toll. It seemed just about everything I did I changed; every drive was carefully driven in my head before taking the best route on the road. I found myself not taking showers until someone was home, because what if I slipped and hit my head and passed out? I couldn't even clean myself without worry or fear! I was miserable.

It was a very dark time that changed to a darker shade of black with everything about me. The momxiety was grueling, but I had no choice. I couldn't live with myself if I didn't listen to a thought. At times, I felt it was divine intervention speaking to me. And if I didn't listen, I was doomed for bad things to happen, and it scared the crap out of me.

By now, everyone, knew about my anxiety and panic struggles. My mom was aware, and not visiting her as much as I used to was very hard on me, and I'm sure her. We did talk on the phone a lot, but due to my fear of driving, I lost precious time seeing her. Something I would later regret.

I lost a lot of time worrying and redirecting my life around my anxiety and momxiety. Even though I had to, and it made it easier for me to not go into full panic mode. I was surviving the best I could but felt like a crazy maniac otherwise.

The only thing that was good out of this is my daughter doesn't remember her mom being this way, because she was too little. I am very thankful and grateful for that silver lining, but regretful for the good and normal that I had missed, too.

CHAPTER NINE

IT WAS ME ALL ALONG.

I feel like my life was hanging just over rock bottom. Each day filled with constant worry, anxiety over my life, momxiety over my daughter, mixed with panic episodes and debilitating thoughts, I needed an answer to what the hell was wrong with me. I felt the answer, that I wished for daily, would be the key to setting me free from what whatever grips that held on to me and was controlling my life.

These were the darkest days of my life, but they shouldn't have been, because I should be cherishing these precious days with our daughter and our little family.

I know there was some post-partum depression going on, too. I was getting overwhelmed with Kyla's crying. I know that sounds so horrible, but it truly wasn't her or her crying at all. It was my mountain of issues that were beginning to topple over. Yes, I did see my doctor, and no I didn't want to go on medication again. I just dug my toes in and tried to weather the storm that was already knocking me around.

I have pleaded to find an answer. Between Doctors, Specialists, and Fire Department personnel, I would ask what is wrong with me, to no avail. I would talk to my mom, who just encouraged me to think positive and not dwell on the negative. Wise words, but they fell on deaf ears.

I even prayed. I prayed for an answer, and by this point, a good or bad answer. If it were bad, then I knew what was ahead of me. At least I'd have an answer to work with. What was happening in my life suggested to me that something bad was happening, but nobody could find anything! It was one of the loneliest and hopeless feelings I have ever lived in.

I began to feel like this is just the way my life is going to be until my life is over. The joy of life that I once had, and so desperately wanted back, was now just a memory, and as I accepted this, I felt incredibly sad and lifeless.

My shoulders that were hung by my earlobes from stress and anxiety, were beginning to shrug forward as I felt my head begin to hang down. I didn't stand tall in confidence like I felt I had before. Nope. It was everything I could do to just survive a twenty-four-hour period of my life; I just did my best to be upright that day.

Kyla was such a great baby, aside from the crying, and each day I could expect a smile from my face because of her. She kept me from caving in and staying in bed to just let the day pass me by. Besides, her cute little face, and ringlet curls were always worth me investing my time in her. I strived to be the best mom to her, even in my state of anxiety. Some days I'd come close to being what I imagined as the best mom to her, others were not-so-good. But I did what I felt was my best each day to try to be the best mom and the idea of fixing myself and finding that answer grew greater in strength.

Kyla was on a schedule that would usually have me feeding her after midnight. So, I would get up, head out to the living room, and turn on the TV and feed her until she fell asleep again.

This one particular night, I had stayed up a little later than I expected. I found the majority of what was on television was infomercials, and while they can reel you in, I was just over watching them and began to see what else was on.

I stumbled across this one infomercial that caught my attention, I watched for a second, then changed the channel again, only to have my mind say, "wait a minute, what was she saying?" I changed back to this informercial and watched in pure awe of what I was hearing.

They were talking about stress, depression, anxiety and...panic attacks. This group of people, from all different walks of life where explaining what was happening in their bodies, the symptoms that were identical to mine. They talked about the fears they had— driving, being in crowded areas, having to be near exits, I was like, "yes! Me too!" They spoke about nearly *everything* I was dealing with in my life. There was only one catch, "call in for a free tape to hear more and learn about our program" and then it went into the selling of a tape set. I was skeptical right away. Even though I had heard so much about myself and what was going on, I wasn't, "buying" the whole sales pitch and let my skepticism talk me out of being fooled.

But there was a strong sense of interest of what was on that tape. It was free, after all, what could it hurt by getting a free tape? Naturally, my anxiety spoke up and put a negative spin on that answer. But is this my answer? What if I don't get the tape, and it could help me out of this black hole of despair and negativity? I went to bed with the number written down for the free tape in my living room, and for once in a very long time, a level of comfort in knowing what I just heard, finally offered some relief. For me, when you hear of someone talking about the same exact things you are going through, the relatability lowers the vibration of anxiety and negativity, because you don't feel like you're the only one going through this. Heck, I just saw and heard five people going through what I have been going through at one time. That's a huge sigh of relief!

The next morning, I ordered the tape. I called in and felt awkward talking to a call center representative about this order, and nearly hung up the phone while doing so. But I didn't, and my tape was on its way.

I recall being upbeat that day and related it to what I had heard on the TV the night before. While the thread of anxiety and momxiety existed, it wasn't vibrating at its normal high rate of volume. I thought about what people said, and how it truly spoke to me directly. I felt I was supposed to be watching that informercial that night. Maybe this is the answer to my prayers, because at this point, every appointment I have been to at this point gave me no satisfaction of what was going on with me. The people on TV did.

After a few days, the tape arrived. I pulled it out of its thick manila mailer and looked at it as if it were gold. I had no idea what this tape would offer me, but there was excitement attached to my thoughts about it. However, I did think to myself to not get too excited, as I don't want to be disappointed and back to square one if this fails my expectations.

The only tape player I had was in my car, and I needed to go to the grocery store and to Keith's parents that day. I got Kyla ready, loaded her up and we were off, with the tape playing. What I noticed right away with the tape not even playing, is I was okay to be driving. Something that hasn't happened in a long time.

I was in complete utter shock and awe as to what I heard on this tape. I remember nodding my head yes, saying yes out loud and finding myself laughing with near tears in my eyes going, this is *me*! Everything about this tape, what everyone was saying and explaining was one hundred percent me. This was my answer. While the doctors would label me with an anxiety and panic disorder, they couldn't explain what this tape has explained to me. Why this was happening. I found out my, "WHY!"

I believe I was meant to find that informercial that early morning as I fed Kyla. While I was so apprehensive to move forward in getting this tape, I was happy I didn't listen to my anxiety and skepticism that hijacked my thoughts.

I did order the tape series, still with a tad of skepticism, but again, was happy I did. I bought a little tape player and went to town listening to each tape as I was instructed to. After two weeks, I felt life breathing back into my body. I felt happy again, with an eagerness to do things and dare I say it, I smiled a bit more, too! I felt like I was walking out of a fog, releasing myself from the grips of the evil holding me back, everything I didn't want to be a part of, but was given what I felt was a life sentence of for no reason.

After two weeks, I didn't have a panic attack again—well, not for a long time, but this time, I knew what it was and didn't bolt from the house with 911 on the phone. I worked through it and calmed myself down.

You see, I was causing *all* of this myself. Say what? I know, but yes, it was me. I was allowing fears, negative self-talk, and body symptoms to take over my life and running with the fear of it all because I didn't know what was causing it, other than some unearthed illness that would eventually be my demise. No, it was not having the tools and understanding of how to calm myself, answer my own fears with real questions and take inventory of what is around me to ground myself. It was also learning that I would be okay in what I was going through. They said, "nobody has died because of a panic attack." For some reason, it took the fear of dying while having one right out of the attack. It was also hearing how each person had exactly the same thing happening in their life, and how they worked through it. It inspired me to write this book. I want people to relate and find their answer and take comfort in knowing they are not alone. Us anxiety and momxiety sufferers need to stick together.

The tape series also taught me self-care, and exercise. If you don't recall, I loved food while being pregnant with Kyla. I weighed 199 pounds the day before I had Kyla. I was a size 8 when I got pregnant. I *really* loved my food.

With following this series and putting time and energy into myself, I started eating healthier and doing yoga. I began to love yoga, even with a crawling Kyla finding my poses as an obstacle course for her to sneak under, but it gave me peace and a good workout at the same time.

By the time Kyla turned one, I was a size four, hundred twenty-eight-pound happy person with her life back in place. While I wasn't the same Jen as before, I was a new and improved version of myself. Did I have anxiety and momxiety still? Yes! Did I still worry? Of course! Did I still think negative and fear things? Oh, heck yes! Did I let them stop me? No way! I found that once I knew it was me causing my own hell, I had every answer I needed! There have been times where I've even whispered to myself, "Jen, shut up and knock it off!"

And being a mom will never silence the momxiety within, in fact, I have found that having anxiety and momxiety is a good thing. Yes— you read that right! You can't not have anxiety in your life, it's very natural. Just sometimes it can get out of control in a bad way. I feel for me, having momxiety allows me to think in a non-mom way for their safety and security. While I'm what you would call a hover mom from years of anxiety, I don't feel it's a bad thing for me. Do I have an imagination that is quite vivid and over the top? Yep, sure do! Do I go to the dark places of thought as I face a situation? Yes—and you have no idea what my mind can come up with.

However, I can control what I respond to. That is the major difference. I can respond in a fearful way and turn negative quickly and be in a panic attack in no time flat. Or, I can ask myself why I am thinking this way and answer my negative questions with positive answers. For example, driving to my mom's. It was jammed packed with fear and controlling thoughts about passing out and something bad happening. Now, I drive there, still with a little anxiety, but I answered my fears. What if I pass out? Well, I'll have a little warning with body symptoms, so I will pull over and call for help. What if something bad happens? My answer—what if nothing bad happens? And if it does, I will get through it the best I can. It takes the sting out of the negative self-talk.

We all have the ability to help ourselves and take back the controlling thoughts and mindsets of our life. Our mind is a very powerful thing, and when used in a positive way, can influence the rest of your life to follow suit. I got lost in negativity, but I found myself with positivity and love for myself. I took care of myself for the first time in my life and found happiness from within. Something I didn't know I had until I was greeted with anxiety and panic disorder.

CHAPTER TEN

HERE WE GO AGAIN

My life seemed to be good since I found out what was wrong with me. Kyla was growing up successfully, crawling to walking, which she decided to do just around eleven months old, and all around being her cute and silly self.

We moved into our second home being a married couple with a child, we were adulting successfully, too. Keith was still working at the Chevrolet Dealer in the parts department, and I started to find a liking for creating things, so I started a small business that sold ATV Apparel for infants and toddlers.

We were traveling more, sometimes without Kyla, and on those occasions, I would have extreme Momxiety. I worried about her in a car with another person, what if they got into an accident? I worried about her sleeping. What if she didn't wake up? I also worried about the house she was in, what if it catches fire and she doesn't get out? Momxiety was alive and well!

One trip, she stayed with my mom, at our house while Keith and I, and our friends Frank and Stacie took the train to Portland, Oregon for an overnight stay. When she stayed at our home, I worried a heck of a lot less. I think her being in her element made me feel more comfortable and relaxed, I still worried, but not to the degree of obsession I would normally worry.

The trip down to Oregon was so much fun! It was 105 degrees with humidity, but the train cars were air conditioned and we kept cool with wine and beer. When we arrived in Oregon, we had a car service pick us up and drive us to our hotel. We took in some shopping, dining, and dancing, but I felt completely off once we stepped off the train in Portland. I felt dizzy and an out of touch feeling. It was like I was in a daze but was fully awake. It didn't stop me, or put me into a panic attack, so I just went with it, but wondering what was wrong most of the trip.

Our trip back wasn't as successful, the train broke down, we lost the air conditioning and they ran out of water. I recall thinking the panicked Jen would have lost her mind. Sitting in a hot tube on the tracks with no A/C and no way out, yep! The panic attack would have been one for the record books!

We finally made it home, and after picking up Kyla and squeezing her with kisses, I thought about how I felt down in Portland. I realized it was probably drinking wine on the train, being in the air conditioning then being hit with the humid hot air once we got off the train in Portland. But in the back of my mind, there was an idea to take a pregnancy test. So, I did, and I was pregnant!

I was a little upset at first, because we hadn't planned on having another child, but my husband was so excited! His excitement took me by surprise and my short-lived sadness was replaced with excitement too.

This pregnancy wasn't at all like my first. I had morning sickness which was literally all day. At sixteen weeks, I started to have stomach cramps and what appeared to be contractions and worried intently on losing our baby. I was thankful my full-blown anxiety and panic disorder was at bay because this was a lot of real anxiety and fear in my life. If I felt anxious, I would get up and move, put music on or do some pregnancy yoga. Anything to keep my mind busy.

I found a fond liking of ginger root tablets as they curbed my nausea and thankfully all cramps and contractions were gone. We found out we'd be having a boy, too! Our family of four would be complete in late March 2007.

Our home was graced with the stomach flu at the beginning of February, which hit me first. It was a full-on flu with all the fixings. I laid there in between bathroom trips, freezing then hot, and the body aches were so severe, it hurt just to touch any part of my skin. I called my friend, Kate, who instructed me to call my doctor. The office said I should go into the hospital because I could start becoming dehydrated and that isn't good at all for me or the baby.

I asked Kate if she could take me, as Kyla was starting to show signs of being sick herself. It wasn't long into the car trip that I tossed my cookies into a Tupperware bowl I brought along, just in case. I felt so much better, but Kate insisted on getting me to the hospital. I was instructed to go to Labor and Delivery since I was pregnant, and they could monitor our little guy, too. It was a good thing I went into the hospital, I was having contractions at 31 weeks, and they needed to give me medication to stop them. I was very dehydrated and needed an IV, and I was able to get anti-nausea medication, too. I was concerned about the medications I was being prescribed, since my fear of medication was still intact.

I was admitted into the hospital for observation, and Kate stayed the night with me. She also brought me the best grape popsicle I have ever had in my entire life; it was so juicy and refreshing.

Our little slumber party was another test to my recovery. Keith and Kyla stayed home, and unfortunately Kyla ended up vomiting all over our bed at 2am, so my husband was up doing laundry all night. I was concerned over her all night, and I missed my husband. I sincerely didn't want to be in the hospital but had no choice. The medication they gave me for my contractions was making my heart race like I had just ran a marathon, my heartbeats were always a major anxiety trigger, and it was making me uncomfortable. They also gave me a sleeping pill, which I found out happens to wire me. I was wide awake all night. I was jealous of Kate who was over on the couch sleeping in such peace. The whole situation was very uncomfortable for me, and I had to keep my mind out from the hole of negativity that I seemed to be tipping toward. I told myself I was in a hospital, so I should be feeling, "safe" and that helped to relax me some.

Just after I was released, I was put on bedrest for contractions again at 32 weeks. Bedrest? And furthermore, *me* being on bedrest? You have got to be kidding me? I move to keep from being anxious, I wasn't a sit around the house type of person anyway, I liked to go shopping, to the craft store and grocery store. I don't sit well by any means and now the forceful act was stirring up what if's all over the place.

I was fortunate enough to have a great team of people to help me, because being on bedrest alone was difficult, but having a toddler was another issue. Between Keith, my mom and my dear friend, Kate, I had help each and every day. They cleaned my house, did laundry, my grocery shopping and made meals. And furthermore, they had to be stern with me, because it was making me feel awful for them having to do all of this for me. I felt guilty, but I couldn't jeopardize our son's life just to fold a basket of laundry. I laughed at myself many times because I'd begin to feel depressed and helpless, even though I had all the help in the world around me. Again, it's simply amazing what your mind can create when it has time to travel.

I fell into a routine of watching shows on TV, taking showers because at least I was upright for a few minutes and I got good at crossword puzzles. Kyla loved having the company and especially grandma loving on her and giving into her finger points for snacks and treats that she wanted. This is when it hit me that Kyla won't be the center of attention in our lives anymore. I wasn't able to hold her, pick her up or snuggle with her because of my pregnancy and bedrest and I felt I was intentionally not giving her attention, and I was worried she would feel the effects of this, too. Kyla and I were two peas in a pod, and to feel like I was constantly saying, "no honey," and

"I'm sorry, I can't," or "go see Dad, Grandma or Kate," I was giving her reason to believe I didn't want her around me.

As the weeks were passing, my anxiety grew with my belly. I was to have another c-section because of my first birth, and it was also hospital policy at that time. Again, fine by me, but on an excruciating level, I was terrified of going into surgery and something horrible go wrong. I was up against a birth and momxiety of, "what if's," and a son that wanted to make his entrance into this world before his due date.

CHAPTER ELEVEN

ANXIOUSLY WAITING.

At 36 weeks pregnant, I found myself in labor and delivery at Good Samaritan Hospital. My doctor was available for phone calls, but was not on call or in the area, which immediately spiked any normalcy in my mind during this anxious time. I craved knowing, and hated surprises, something post anxiety and panic disorder has left in its wake.

I was given the medication to slow things down and surprisingly sent home by my doctor. I was instructed to come back if things were to pick up again and to try and relax and find some comfort, he was also back in the area the next day.

My mom had taken me to the hospital, Keith and Kyla stayed back to see what the next steps were, and to get things prepared in case it was truly time to meet our son. When we were released, my mom asked me if I was hungry and given the chance to eat in a restaurant after being on bedrest for so long, I undoubtably chose Olive Garden for their pasta, breadsticks, and soup. I was going all out on this meal! Besides, it could be one of my last outings before I'm a mom of two and given some time to be with my mom was rewarding because our bond was so strong, and her presence was something I always thoroughly enjoyed. And just in case you're wondering, I ate until I couldn't eat another bite that night. I was happy to have home cooked meals—and Keith's grilled cheese sandwiches were seriously the best dinners we had. I usually did the cooking, so to have him cook was wonderful, but I soon found his secret ingredient, a ton of butter.

My mom stayed the night at our home, and it was good that she did. Around mid-morning, I was having contractions and I decided to call my doctor's office, who instructed me to go into the hospital.

Keith was at work, and kept in touch with me, it wasn't any use for him to come to the hospital if they were going to give me medication and then send me on my way again.

Today was different, though. I was 36 weeks and one day along in my pregnancy and when Dr. Romig came in, with full scrubs and a hat on, holding a box of Thin Mint Girl Scout cookies, he said, "today you're having a baby." It just all got real. Plus, I wanted a damn cookie now and couldn't due to my c-section.

I went from a little anxious to full on, momxiety about leaving Kyla when I went into surgery. I was not mentally prepared and now I was fast approaching surgery and a birth in a matter of hours. I was not okay with this one bit.

I called my friend Kate to let her know and she came down to the hospital. This birth wasn't the fanfare Kyla's was. This time, it was Keith, Kyla, my Mom and Kate. Nobody else. Keith's parents flew out to Hawaii that morning, and other family members were working or in college.

It was decided that Kate and Keith would go into the OR with me, and my mom would stay with Kyla in my room to keep her occupied and see if she could get her to nap a bit. It was bittersweet because of course you want your mom in situations like this, but I was happy knowing I didn't have to worry about Kyla, too. Besides, Kate is a wonderful friend, so with her and Keith with me, I knew I was in good hands.

It was time for me to walk to the Operating room and I literally lost it. I cried holding onto Kyla and hugging her. I was terrified it would be the last time I saw her, and I just didn't want to do this. I hated the fact that I was so scared and not taking in a moment that was so good and happy. Another after effect of anxiety and panic disorder—I felt I had to worry in case, because if I'm not worrying, something bad could happen. I wiped away my tears and gave one last hug to my mom and Kyla and did my best to smile before I walked out of my room towards the operating room.

After enduring the high spinal from Kyla's birth, I alerted the anesthesiologist of what happened before, with a chuckle, he did his job beautifully and this time, I wasn't gripping my tongue between my teeth when Kate and Keith walked in.

The energy in the Operating room was light and airy, the nurses and Dr. Romig were cracking jokes and he double checked with me that I did want my tubes tied after our son was born. I exclaimed, Heck yes! I was happy to have two children, and to not have to go through this anxiety again.

Before long, I heard the cry of our son. Evan Patrick was born on Friday, March 2' 2007 at 4:04pm weighing seven pounds thirteen ounces and nineteen and a half inches long. For being a month early, he was a big boy! He was quickly whisked away and cleaned up and brought over to Keith who brought his plump little face down to me on the operating table.

After I was able to meet him, the nurses took Keith and Evan to get him cleaned up, take him to the window to see Kyla and my mom, but he was having some blood sugar problems and needed to have some extra attention. Keith came into the recovery room to let me know, and of course that worried me, but he assured me it was because he was early and is sort of a normal thing.

I was wheeled back into our room to catch the last twenty minutes of Oprah, and Evan joined not long after. Keith took my mom and Kyla home for a bit to clean up and grab a bite and some snacks for Kyla at the Hospital. I slept and was very happy to. I was a ball of nerves and the downside of all that expended energy was exhaustion, a feeling I recall all too well.

Evan was able to be with us in our Hospital room and not in the NICU, which I was thankful for. His blood sugars evened out and he was eating like a champ, too. A new worry for this mom to add to her momxiety list was a baby with possible blood sugar issues. I know he was better, but what if he did have issues? How would I recognize them? What if something happened when he was sleeping, and I didn't catch it? My sister is a diabetic, and I know she'd be a wealth of information if he did indeed have a blood sugar issue, but at the same point, I wanted Evan to be healthy. His pregnancy was filled with a lot of fear with all the contractions that seemed to have started around sixteen weeks. My mom explained it frankly to me one day, that he's a fighter and he's here! A lot could have gone wrong, but you're holding him. Enjoy it.

Why so simple are the words, but so difficult is the action of them? She was right. I should be enjoying him and our sweet little family, instead of worrying about what if's and his health. Yes, he did have a blood sugar issue, but it was one time, right after his birth, and it was corrected quickly. Instead I was labeling him a diabetic and frantic about the care that would go into that, my worry truly had no merit.

As the afternoon gave way to night, I snuggled with Kyla and Evan in my hospital bed and watched TV with Keith. Our little family was complete. Two beautiful healthy kids, a loving and kind husband and me, a less worried version of my former self. Life was evolving anxiety and momxiety or not. It was still my choice where my path would go, and in that moment, I choose happiness over worry. It was a beautiful moment.

CHAPTER TWELVE

WHEN THE "WHAT IF'S" COME MARCHING IN

For this post surgery, now mom of two, I sure had experience after experience that elevated momxiety to new levels. The recovery from my second c-section was rough. It started when I was still in the hospital, when I sipped my water through a straw, and it went down the wrong pipe and I coughed. Coughing post c-section dropped me to my knees, and the unsuccessful attempt to stop myself from coughing just drove the pain even further.

The cough caused something to move, shift or split, because I was having a hard time moving my right leg because it was pulling on my stomach muscles, and from that point on, it was game on with pain and suffering.

To show the difference in my c-sections, I didn't fill the pain prescription with Kyla's birth, I only used Tylenol. Evan's, I filled the prescription and requested a refill. I'm sure having my tubes tied was another difference in recovery, but I was down for the count for several weeks after his birth. The only upswing was having Keith make those heart stopping grilled cheese sandwiches and ordering take out from our favorite Mexican restaurant. It appeared that my bedrest wasn't over after all.

Evan was the opposite of Kyla, he was awake three times a night, and each night around six o'clock, he would start crying and not stop for a couple hours. It turns out, the formula wasn't his friend and he had so much gas he herniated his belly button. I felt awful. Why didn't I notice this was happening? My momxiety was allowing me to feel like I was a bad mother, and I just let my infant suffer at my hands. My negativity was intoxicating, and it led me to feel completely down about myself. Add sleep deprivation, a newborn and active toddler to the mix, I was a hot mess, and could see my heartbeat on the outer corner of my eyes each day. Which sent me running to my phone to call my doctor. Having anxiety doesn't allow for in the moment, realistic thinking. You have to get an answer to what is happening before you can move on and feel confident in what is really going on at hand and understand it. I was dipping into some postpartum depression and with not having a good night's sleep, I was exhausted, and my body was showing signs of it. Which turns into momxiety after I'm done worrying about myself and my own health concerns. The "what if's" came marching in. What if I'm so tired I accidently hurt my kids? What if I fall asleep and Kyla is roaming around the house and does something accidently? What if I fall while holding Evan because I'm so tired and clumsy and we get hurt? Being in my state of mind wasn't allowing me to understand that this is a moment in life and would pass. I have a newborn and a two-year-old. That alone is a lot but recovering from surgery with complications just adds to the mix of emotions happening.

Our poor little Evan was giving mom major momxiety with his first few weeks of birth. He had to go under the lights for jaundice and was having circulation problems that would turn his feet and lower legs a blackish purple color when you held him. I hated to leave him at the hospital, and worried about him being alone under the lights. I felt so bad for Evan. I started to feel guilty for having him a month early. Could I have done better during my pregnancy? The swirls of blame and negative self-talk was beginning to chip away at me.

In the midst of my emotional roller coaster, our sweet daughter, Kyla was trying to help mom one day and picked up Evan and accidently dropped him. I had laid him on the couch, went to grab something in the kitchen and heard the thud and instant crying. She wanted to hold him but being so little herself at just over two years old, she couldn't balance herself and he fell to the floor and appeared to have injured his shoulder. I certainly wasn't mad at Kyla, but I was very concerned about Evan because each time I touched that shoulder area, he screamed in pain.

I grabbed both my kids and took off fiercely to the doctor's office where we were directed to get an X-ray. I was a wreck, this poor kid! It appeared he was just having a rough start to his little life. I will never forget the x-ray for him. It brings tears to my eyes just thinking about it. Because he was so little, and wiggly, they had to secure him in this chair of sorts, that had a plastic mold that fit around his body and his poor little arm had to be lifted straight above his head. The pure pain, dread and fear coming from my Evan as he looked at me with big tears rolling down his cheeks, was the worst thing I have ever seen one of my kids go through. Then I had to leave the room for the x-ray. I leaned up against the wall and used the wall to fall to the floor in tears. I completely unraveled on the floor. Kyla sat beside me quietly, and it made me feel bad for her, too. I know she didn't mean any of this, and I was not the mom she has known all her life in that moment. She saw the other side of me, the anxious momxiety side of me, something I try to ban from my kid's life.

Evan's X-ray from hell session was over and my sweet little boy was convulsing with tears as I picked him up and snuggled him. I kept saying I was sorry, and the x-ray techs were consoling me saying, "Mom, it's okay, you're a good mom, accidents happen." Surely the thought of me being investigated for hurting my child was a fear I had, too. I would never hurt my child in any way but having someone question my ability of being a great mom now entered into my realm of thinking and opened up a new avenue of fear to travel down, once again.

Thankfully Evan was just fine, appeared to have some soreness though, but nothing broken. The day of shopping I had planned sure sounded better than what actually played out, but we were home, happy, exhausted, and ready to just let the day fade out.

Our kids were our world, Keith and I introduced them to our activities, which included camping and going to the sand dunes. We didn't stop having fun, but rather allowed our kids and our family to start traditions early and make memories at a small age. Now being older, they do remember camping trips and road trips. They talk about learning to ride quads at an early age, and places they like to revisit over and over again.

Keith and I had decided when I was pregnant with Kyla that I would be a stay-at-home-Mom and he would work full time. It was so rewarding, and I was blessed to be able to do that for our family.

I don't know what I would have done with my momxiety if I worked and they were in someone else's care. I was that mom who only let family watch our kids. It was usually my mom; she was single and loving on her grandkids was a number one priority for her. Keith parents watched them at times, but for the most part, my mom would come over on a Friday and stay the weekend. It was a huge blessing as my mom would step in to keep the kids occupied while Keith and I straightened up the house—my husband is a meticulous guy and loves to clean, even doing dishes and laundry. I scored with this guy!

It was always great spending time with my mom, because I felt safe with her around, too. Of course, Keith was home, so it was an all-around safe two and a half days of stress and anxiety free time. It was like I was on a vacation from my inner thoughts and my worries. I always looked forward to the weekends.

Kyla and Evan were growing each day, and poor little Evan was still battling through his issues. He was diagnosed with eczema at just one years old and had what appeared to be cradle cap so bad that nothing, but olive oil saved him. My mom was the one who used the oil one day, and after prescriptions weren't working, we were willing to try anything. We'd grease up his little head and put him in his highchair and let him eat before giving him a bath. Oh, the pictures I have of him with what little hair he had left going in multiple directions.

It seemed to be one thing after another and suffering from momxiety was not letting up, in fact, I thought them being little was anxious enough, but having to deal with real and medical situations was sometimes too much for this mama to endure.

I know we all worry about our kids, but this period of time sure made its impression. While I am thankful for their health and the, "good news" that came out of hectic and stressful situations we were in at times, it came at a cost of my stress and anxiety. Worth it? Every time! Just happy the little infant x-ray days are over.

CHAPTER THIRTEEN

BRICK WALL

A test to my recovery with panic and anxiety disorder was a road trip to Reno. Being in a car with no cell phone service at times was enough to send me unpacking our suitcases. However, my interest in testing my recovery was far more motivating. I was spreading my wings instead of trying to play it safe and it became encouraging to see myself be so courageous.

Since my recovery, there's been a lot of differences in the way I navigated life. I used to pack for a trip in three minutes and fly by the seat of my pants. Now, it's a week-long process of to-do lists, organized chaos and the last-minute grocery store or target trip to get, "EVEYRTHING" I just may need, because you know, there isn't any sort of store along the way on our trip.

Our first major trip as a family was to celebrate my mom's sixtieth birthday and spread her mom's ashes in the Truckee River in Downtown Reno. This trip also was the second trip for me and my siblings with my mom, the first is when we were much younger, multiple decades ago. So much good was going into this trip and celebration and I allowed myself to feel that excitement, and process it as excitement, not fear that would cue the negative thinking and start me down the path of panic. My recovery was everything to me, and proving to myself I was indeed, okay, had a life changing impact.

The drive to and from Reno was wonderful. No anxiety, no discomfort of fear or vibrations of nervousness. The scenery and conversations with my husband and kids kept everything positive, plus my brother, sister and our mom were following in the car behind us most of the way down, so it was a distraction, too.

I did have a day of nervous anxiety, and it truly bugged me so much that I was annoyed with being anxious. I felt I was all inside my body, my eyes were tunnels and I felt weak and clumsy. When I get anxious, I get fidgety, so I was looking like a cracked-out person moving and making what felt like uncontrolled twitches, but it wasn't really that. My husband would always say it looks like I'm on drugs when I get fidgety. Well, in some cases I was, the drug I created in my head that sent me to another realm in this world, and it would hit you like a brick wall. Moving made me feel better —because I was getting stuck energy and adrenaline out of my body.

I managed to get through that anxiety episode and move to a much happier mentality as we celebrated mom's sixtieth and captured memories in our minds and on camera. Those photograph memories would soon have a greater sense of meaning.

Our trip ended successfully all around. Our kids had a lot of fun, we came out ahead from gambling, we made it home safe and I did this entire trip with hardly any anxiety or one panic attack! I felt my dedication to overcoming anxiety has been a struggle at times, but by far, this was a life changing moment for me as I was able to prove to myself otherwise. I can do it and allow myself to deal with anxiety as it comes and extinguish its role in my life by living it out and not unpacking my thoughts there to increase its intensity. If I could face myself and say how proud I was and give a hug with that warm pat on the back, I would have. I was that happy. I feel I could face anything and be okay. Little did I know the greatest challenge and test to my recovery was going to stare me down to the greatest depths of the unknown.

Celebrating mom's sixtieth was a lot of fun, but it was strange to think of my mom being sixty. Thankfully she was happy, had the best sense of humor and the kindest regard for others and paid forward acts of kindness. She was everything to me, and her sudden death not only shook me to the core of existence but sent me and everyone she knew into complete shock and a level of sadness I didn't know could occur.

On September 19, 2009, my family and I went to my mom's house, so she could watch our kids while we went to Ikea. Normally she would be at our home on the weekends, but for some strange reason, we took the trip to see her.

I had the strangest feeling on the way to her house. I turned to my husband and said, "I feel like something good is going to happen to me in my future." It was like I was given a peak into my future for a split second and could feel that happiness, but once that feeling faded, I felt uneasy and flat out different. I couldn't peg it, but soon I would know why I was feeling this way.

When we arrived at my mom's house, I grabbed Kyla from her car seat and headed up the stairs to my mom's door at her condo. I knocked, but nobody answered. Weird, but maybe she was in the bathroom. So, I used my key to open her door. Once inside, I felt she wasn't even home. It was clean, quiet and no lights were on. When I walked near the kitchen, I could see my mom's feet on the floor, then her legs and it was then I knew something was terribly wrong. I screamed, "Holy Shit, MOM!" She didn't reply. She was lying face down on the carpet with her glasses by her side. She was alive, but unable to speak to tell us what happened. We raced to call 911 and attend to her. I took Kyla and Evan and ran to the street to wait for the ambulance. Keith stayed with her and assured her we were getting her help and that we loved her.

When she was being attended to, the paramedics put her on her back and they tried to lift her left arm and leg, it was if the bones were stripped from her skin as they just fell to the floor, limp. She had suffered a stroke and needed medical attention fast.

She was taken my ambulance to the hospital, my brother Kyle met me there first. My sister Val and my brother Ryan would soon meet us, too.

She was taken to CAT scan and was told she needed to be intubated because she stopped breathing. My mom was in critical condition, and it was found she had suffered a large aneurysm. She was on life support and was fighting for her life.

On September 24th, 2009, six days after her aneurysm, my mom, my truest best friend, and the person who gave me life, died with her family surrounding her at the Hospital.

My head hung, and my body felt heavy. My mom just died was something looping in my head. At home, I looked at the pictures we took in Reno. My mom was smiling, she was having a great time, and most of all, she was alive. I didn't have a lot of pictures of my mom prior to the trip, so the value was priceless in them now.

The test to my recovery was looming over my life. For six days I was strong, I was impressed by my strength to carry on and be there for my mom. I didn't really have any bad breakdowns, of course a couple melting crying episodes of disbelief, but nothing panic or anxiety led. I kept asking myself, "why was I doing so good in all of this?"

It wasn't too long before the grief hit. I would literally crash on my kitchen floor with a bottle wine and sob. I found that hurt and pain of losing someone could turn into physical pain. I began drinking wine to escape from the pain. Like a large liter bottle and at times, I would drink a regular bottle after the liter was gone. I wasn't really suffering from any anxiety or panic attacks, it was more pain from missing my mom, and disbelief that she is truly gone, and she wouldn't be coming back.

The one thing I had to do is keep myself busy, so I wouldn't regress into my role of anxiety and panic attack sufferer. I knew the dark world of anxiety, and mom's death was a deeper shade of black that had no level of depth. I knew in my heart I couldn't go back to suffering, I needed to stay in the recovery side.

Losing my mom could have easily sent me to bed for weeks, not caring about my life, my kids, or my husband. I could have feared about my own health, since having a stoke was a main trigger of mine, but I didn't. I could have lost my mind, easily, I could have lost my life, but I couldn't.

I was learning so much about myself with my mom's death and learning more about my anxiety and panic disorder recovery. I learned that I was strong, and able to move forward, if it meant I got out of bed and threw my hair up in a scrunchie and took the day on bra-less.

I was a hot mess for a bit of time, though. My wine-sobbing-kitchen-floor-episodes where nightly for a while. They lessened, and so did the wine drinking, but it was a routine that helped me get through.

I found myself crying for no reason, including hearing a song that brought back memories. I had dark days of just depressive behavior, and a couple runs down a main street after leaving a night club just wanting to be done with this hurt. Thankfully my husband gave chase and saved me. I was emotional, and distraught, and those times scared me. But they have also brought me to the person I am today, so I praise them.

You see, grief is real. I had to internalize my grief and find a way to cope that worked for me. What I rested on was this. The emotional and physical pain I felt in losing my mom was because she truly meant everything to me. My tears and wine-soaked episodes of despair is a result of knowing and having unconditional love. My disbelief and hate of her being in heaven is because of her presence in my life, I always say when I talk about her is that, "she was one of a kind." She truly was.

My recovery was tested beyond a level I can comprehend. But I made it through the darkest time of my life with hardly any anxiety or panic. I suffered from grief, and I'm happy to say that my grief will never go away. I will always miss my mom, and my grief will always be welcomed into my life, it's the process of remembering her.

Hug your mom's and tell them you love them. I envy those who still can and relate to those who look up to the heavens and say, "Mom, I wish I could hug you right now."

CHAPTER FOURTEEN

MOMXIETY CLUB

A lot of life has been spent since my first panic attack. Looking back, I'm thankful for having anxiety and panic disorder. I hated the scary episodes and the fear, but through it all I grew a strength I didn't know I had, and it has changed my life for the better.

I've learned anxiety can be a good thing in your life. For me, when I begin to feel anxious, I ask myself what is bothering me right now. Usually it's a bit of stress, an upcoming situation, such as my kids going camping with their grandparents, or sometimes having to deal with an individual. There's always an answer to my anxiety.

I've also learned that momxiety will NEVER go away. I have worried about my kids more than I have ever worried about myself. Sadly, I fear this world they are growing up in. Between the bullying, the suicides, the child abductors, sex trafficking, stranger danger, social media, school shootings and mass shootings, my momxiety beacon is constantly going off.

It down right scares the hell out of me. My kid's safety is an obsession of mine, and at times can be overboard, but I don't give one care to someone who thinks I'm overprotective. They do not have to live with this mind of mine if the unthinkable happens because I let my guard down one time to make someone else happy. And I'm proud of being that parent. Sure, I'm could be called a helicopter parent, and that's fine. I will use the blades on my helicopter to cut you out of my life. There's no room for negativity when it comes to my momxiety. And if you're feeling challenged by your momxiety, too, give yourself permission to be proud of who you are and not sacrifice your own peace of mind to make someone else feel validated.

There was this one time I let my guard down and I nearly collapsed when I couldn't find Kyla. We were camping with our friends at a lake. We had a big group of us camping out. We had many activities to do, too, between boating, using the slip and slide they built and riding quads, us adults and our kids were having a great time.

Kyla was playing with Cassie, and then they were gone. Literally, gone. Couldn't find them. I began to check trailers, no sign of them. We all were yelling their names, with no response back. We all began to fear the worst. The lake is here, and I know Kyla doesn't know how to swim. Some went to the lake, others ran around the camp, some took off in their trucks, and then Jason yelled at me to get in his truck. We drove across to this camp that some other friends of theirs was at, and we found Kyla and Cassie there. I jumped out of the truck and ran to her and nearly collapsed with the onset of relief as the adrenaline was still screaming through my entire body. She was safe, and always was, they just went farther than we expected when we had heard they were going to visit Cassie's friend.

I was so pissed at myself for not being a good mom and losing my child while camping. In my mind, Kyla was lost and to not have her respond to any of us was one of the scariest moments of my life. After everything calmed down and Kyla and Evan were hanging out with Keith at the bonfire, I took a few minutes to myself and cried. I sat at the top of the sand dunes overlooking the lake and the sunset and just allowed myself to be sad and be thankful at the same time. My body was still vibrating with adrenaline, and the what ifs were steaming through my head, because this could have easily been a tragic outcome. From that moment on, it was all eyes on the kids, always. Period.

My momxiety has allowed me to be outspoken, because mostly I'm an introvert. I have stood up for myself when before I was the doormat, and its shocked me and the person with whom I've stood up to.

There's no greater confidence than shocking yourself and seeing a positive result, the one you wanted.

Sure, I can be completely crazy with my thoughts about the safety of my kids, but that's on me. I'm okay with looking like a foolish mom, but I have been yet to be proven wrong.

With Kyla being a teen, and Evan soon following, I have future momxiety going on within my mind now. Kyla is close to driving, that's going to be a whole new level of momxiety that I'm not sure I'm ready for. Being mindful of things in the present and the future is a wonderful quality. I believe when you have kids you are agreeing to worry about them your entire lifetime. I knew being pregnant with both of them that I was going to worry about them. Heck, I worried about them in my tummy, why would I stop when they are born?

Honestly, I am surprised by how much goes into being a mom recovering from anxiety and panic disorder. But I wouldn't have it any other way. I have guidelines for my kids' friends. My husband or myself meet their parents and go to the house where our kids will be hanging out. We check in on the kids' phones and internet. We talk about the dangers out there and have had the conversations of what to do in the event of a school or mass shooting. Conversations I never imagined or ever wanted to talk about.

We have expressed our, mostly my momxiety concerns with both of them, and they know their mom is a bit overboard, but they know they will never challenge her, too. Kyla will get upset, and she can be, but she's a teen and I'm the mom who is very imaginative and will always have her safety in mind.

What I'm trying to say is if you suffer from momxiety, I salute you. Some mom's can let their kids roam the neighborhoods, let their kids go to their friends' homes without meeting the parents and take public transportation to malls, fairs and more, and they're okay with that. Sure, I envy their carefree parenting, because it would be nice to not worry, but there is no way in hell my kid would be doing that.

We are a moxiety club that quietly sits wherever we are worrying about our kids and exhaling when we get the call from them that they are home safe from school or have arrived to where they are going intact. We are a momxeity club that worries about them driving, going to college, having a boyfriend or girlfriend, moving out, getting married, all the while thinking of how much older we are getting.

We are a momxeity club that holds lifetime memberships because at the end of the day, we might have suffered or are suffering from anxiety and momxiety, but it will never cease, and we will forever be grateful for being gifted with such a blessing of worry, because our kids are our world and us mom's will never stop loving them, momxiety or not.

Blessings to you momxiety club members!

ABOUT THE AUTHOR

Jen Westby has had her fair share with anxiety and panic disorder. Which still comes and goes. She was mostly recovered until mother-hood and the mother of all anxieties; momxiety hit, and that just brings worry and "what if's" to a whole new level.

Jen and her husband have been married since 2004 and together they have raised their two outstanding children, Kyla and Evan.

As a family, they love to travel, give, hang-out with family and friends and pursue the best times of their lives.

Join my Momxiety & Podcast Group on FB Here

www.ingramcontent.com/pod-product-compliance
Lightning Source LLC
Chambersburg PA
CBHW070117070426
42448CB00040B/3050